GREAT STORE DESIGN

Winners from the
Institute of Store Planners/Visual Merchandising+Store Design
Annual Competition

ROCKPORT
PUBLISHERS

ROCKPORT PUBLISHERS · ROCKPORT, MASSACHUSETTS

First published in the United States of America by:
Rockport Publishers, Inc.
146 Granite Street
Rockport, Massachusetts 01966
Telephone: (508) 546-9590
Fax: (508) 546-7141
Telex: 5106019284 ROCKORT PUB

Distributed to the book trade and art trade in the U.S. by:
North Light, an imprint of
F & W Publications
1507 Dana Avenue
Cincinnati, Ohio 45207
Telephone: (513) 531-2222

Other Distribution by:
Rockport Publishers, Inc.
Rockport, Massachusetts 01966

ISBN 1-56496-113-3

10 9 8 7 6 5 4 3 2 1

Designer: Cardinal Communication Graphics
Editor: Rosalie Grattaroti
Production Manager: Barbara States
Production Assistant: Pat O'Maley
ST Production Editor: Mark Kissling/ST Publications

Printed in Hong Kong

Since its founding nearly one hundred years ago, *Visual Merchandising and Store Design* magazine has reported on trends in store design. In Great Store Design, *the editors of VM+SD have compiled the most significant store projects of 1993 in cooperation with The Institute of Store Planners. These award-winning projects were determined by a panel of ISP members who deliberated over more than one hundred submissions to create this book. They considered the five aspects of great retail design: store planning, visual merchandising, graphics, lighting design, and innovation. The thirty-eight stores you'll find on these pages exemplify the power in those five components.*

The collection of stores that follows runs the gamut of current design trends. You'll see the period looks of the arts and crafts movement and classical era in details and materials. There are also clean, spare designs in metal and glass, painted and stained concrete, and wood — from beautiful veneers and solids to the uncut, untreated variety. You'll also find the latest in store planning and environmental design in the major categories, from department stores to specialty shops, mass merchandisers and entertainment retail.

Great store design is found all around us, in the salvaged keynotes of historic buildings, in renovations, and new designs. The elements mix and mingle, bringing influences and trends from around the world and across cultures to create successful shopping environments — ones that suit the merchandise, the community, and, most importantly, the customer.

In assembling the environments and materials of some of the best, VM+SD offers a volume from which to draw ideas, innovations, and inspiration — not for store planners and designers alone, but for all involved in the beauty and science of selling.

The Editors of VM+SD

TABLE OF CONTENTS

Mark Shale

COUNTRY CLUB PLAZA
KANSAS CITY, MO

Design
CHARLES SPARKS + CO.
WESTCHESTER, IL

The conversion of the freestanding, three-level, 56,000-square-foot specialty department store resulted in a multiuse building with Mark Shale as the international-style centerpiece. The two-level store has a totally movable and interchangeable system of freestanding floor fixtures, perimeter fixtures and hardware, plus one-of-a-kind area rugs, commissioned paintings, furniture, and original photography.

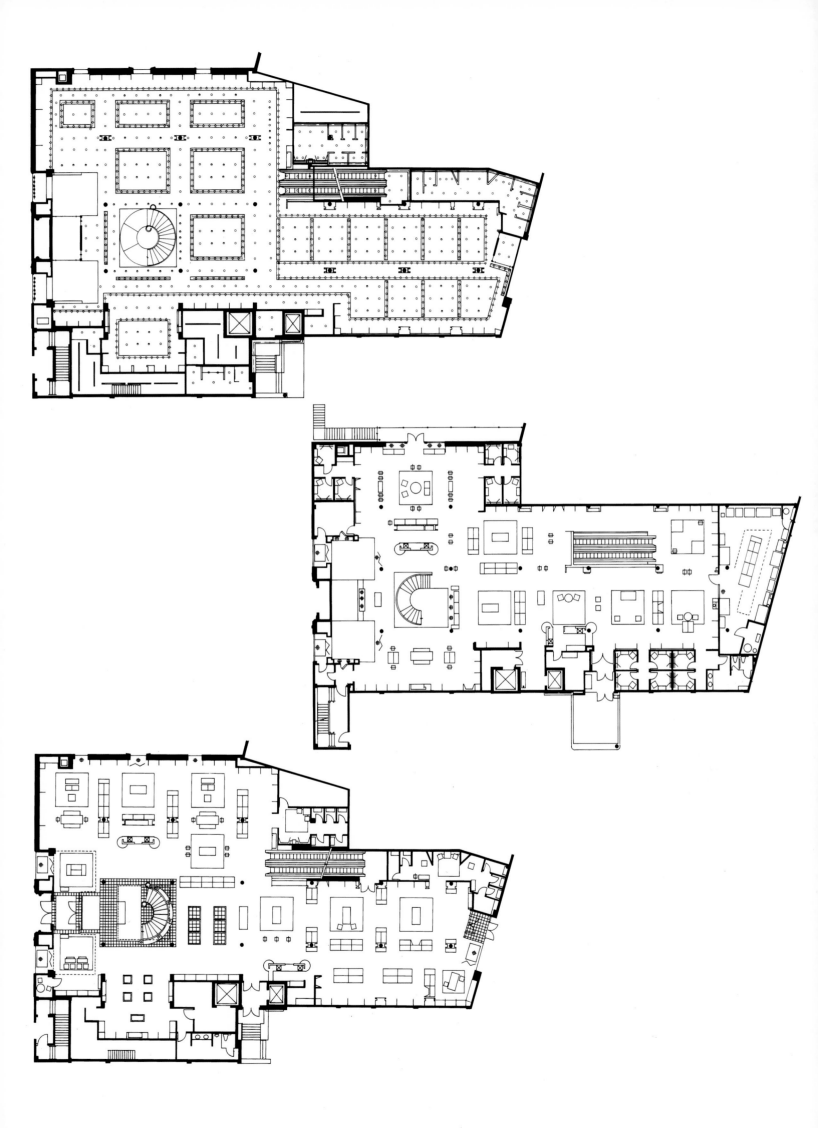

FIRST PLACE

Rich's

NORTH POINT MALL
ATLANTA, GA

Design
HTI/SPACE DESIGN INTERNATIONAL
NEW YORK CITY

With roots in Atlanta since 1867, Rich's newest store makes use of pale colors, natural light, and artwork reflecting current southern state's trends in residential decor.

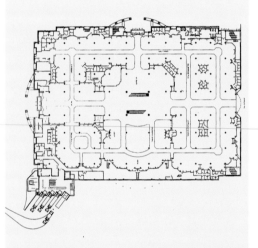

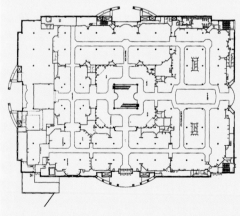

HONORABLE MENTION

Salinas y Rocha

LA GRAN PLAZA
ACAPULCO, MEXICO

Design
SCHAFER ASSOCIATES, INC.
OAKBROOK TERRACE, IL

Salinas y Rocha's new design at La Gran Plaza emphasizes home and family. All design features combine an international look with the influences and materials of Salinas y Rocha's native country.

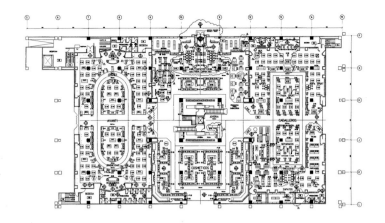

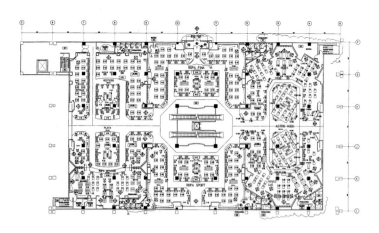

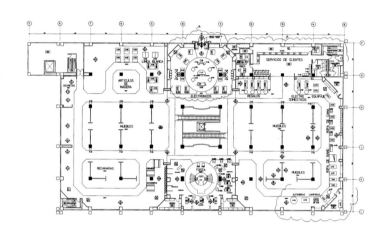

HONORABLE MENTION

Parisian

TOWN CENTER
KENNESAW, GA

Design
WALKERGROUP/CNI
NEW YORK CITY

The new 130,000-square-foot Parisian abandons many stereotypical department store adjacency and fixturing solutions in favor of the flexible design features of specialty stores. In many cases, less dense merchandise and clearly exposed feature areas create a more expensive appearance.

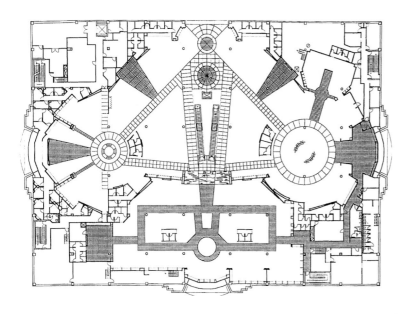

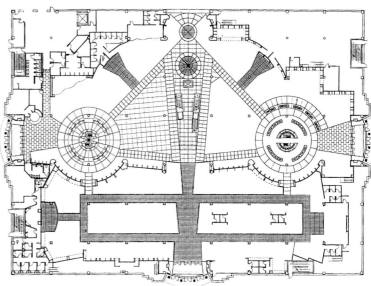

FIRST PLACE

Saks Fifth Avenue

SIXTH FLOOR MEN'S DEPARTMENT
NEW YORK CITY

Design
FITZPATRICK DESIGN GROUP, INC.
NEW YORK CITY

Most dramatic about the renovation of design and merchandising in Saks' men's department is the newly opened windows on the Fifth Avenue side overlooking Rockefeller Plaza. The formal Oval Room and new windows anchor the plan and designer shops now occupy center stage in an environment influenced by surrounding architecture and *art deco.*

HONORABLE MENTION

Saks Fifth Avenue

FIFTH FLOOR MEN'S STORE, UNION SQUARE
SAN FRANCISCO

Design
TUCCI SEGRETE & ROSEN CONSULTANTS INC.
NEW YORK CITY

Clean, simple lines and residential details denote this remodeled Saks' men's department. Gently bowed aisles of Crema Honey marble are complemented by shops accented with polished Black Magic and Verdi granite and a palette of warm West Coast tones and natural fibers.

Bloomingdale's

SECOND FLOOR SPORTSWEAR
NEW YORK CITY

Design
WALKERGROUP/CNI, NEW YORK CITY

For the renovation of Bloomingdale's flagship's second floor, flexible vendor environments allow the retailer to add, subtract, or combine spaces when necessary without destroying the unified architectural elements throughout. Light, natural colors and materials lend a casually elegant, beach house atmosphere.

contemporar
sportswea
y.e.s.

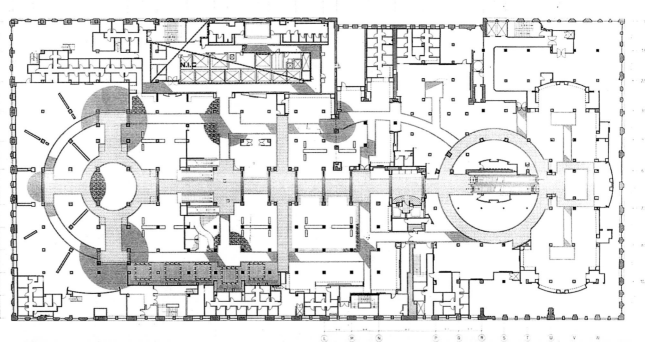

FIRST PLACE

Carson Pirie Scott & Co.

THE SHOPS IN THE MART
MERCHANDISE MART, CHICAGO

Design
SCHAFER ASSOCIATES, INC.
OAKBROOK TERRACE, IL

Carson's new 50,000-square-foot anchor (about half the size of a full-line Carson's) caters to the predominantly professional, adult population at this downtown location. The feel of a specialty store conveys a sophisticated, traditional, urban spirit.

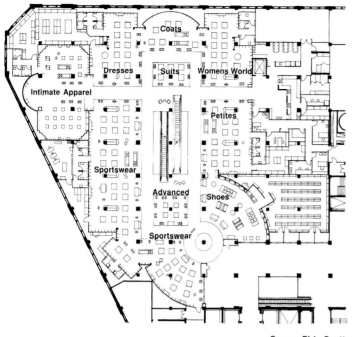

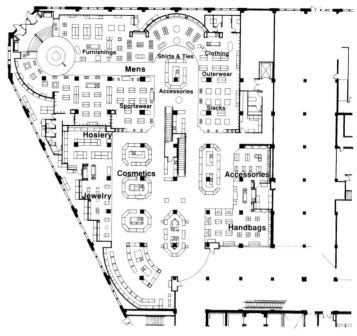

Carson Pirie Scott
Merchandise Mart
Level Two
Chicago, Illinois

Carson Pirie Scott
Merchandise Mart
Level One
Chicago, Illinois

Scott Shuptrine

TROY, MI

Design
JON GREENBERG & ASSOCIATES, INC.
SOUTHFIELD, MI

Once a brown brick furniture showroom, this home fashions store now features eclectic niche presentations, a gray and gold marble walkway and furniture style groups presented on special pods 26 feet in diameter.

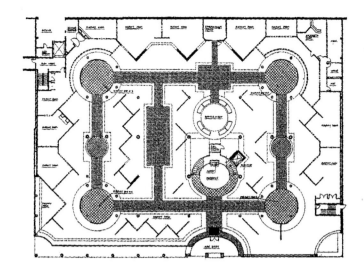
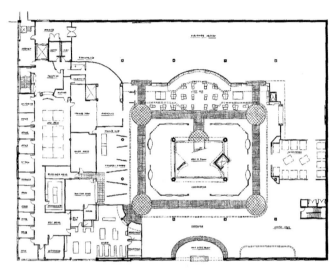

British Home Stores

FRIARS SQUARE SHOPPING CENTER
AYLESBURY, ENGLAND

Design
FITZPATRICK DESIGN GROUP, INC.
NEW YORK CITY

An oval aisle plan paralleled by merchandise walls puts all departments on the aisle with the correct fixture depth in this home furnishings store.

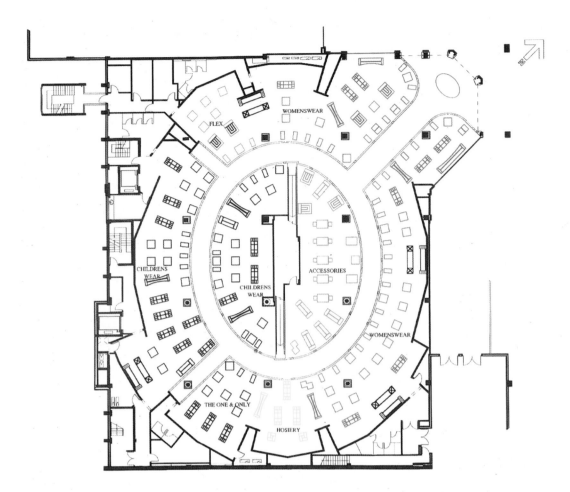

MALL - LAYOUT

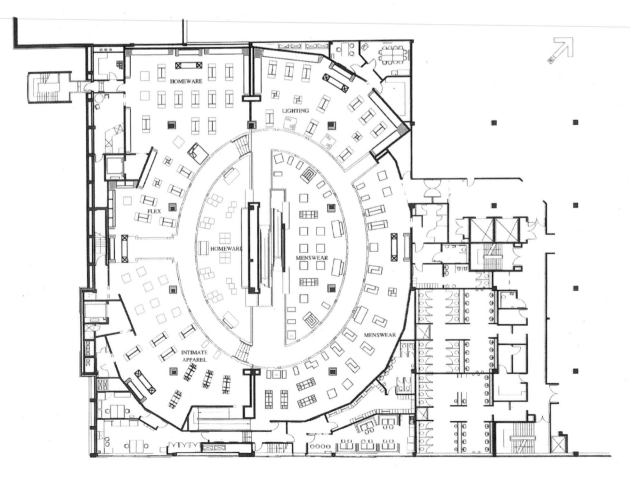

FIRST FLOOR - LAYOUT

FIRST PLACE

La Prairie

INNOVATION AWARD

MAIN FLOOR, BLOOMINGDALE'S
NEW YORK CITY

Design
NORWOOD OLIVER DESIGN ASSOCIATES, INC.
NEW YORK CITY

Switzerland's La Prairie boutique offers a sleek silhouette and hygienically crisp color palette recalling the company's clinical spa heritage boosted by chrome, stainless steel, mirrors and glass, granite, and La Prairie's signature blue. The project was awarded the Innovation Award for a transparent panel that turns opaque for privacy with a flip of a switch

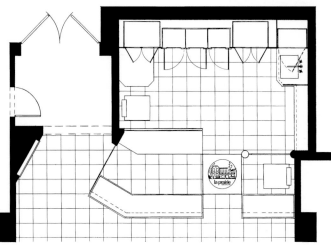

Origins

WEST BROADWAY, NEW YORK CITY

Design
PETER FORBES & ASSOCIATES
BOSTON

Designed with a consciousness of environmental responsibility, this Origins features materials chosen for their durability and non-obsolescence and a storefront window set in pleats to invite passersby to peer in. Crafted to eliminate the "we who know and they who don't" mentality, the shop has no counters separating staff from customers.

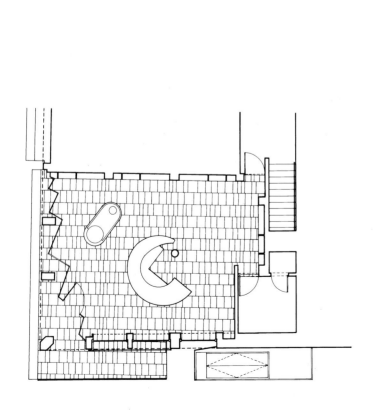

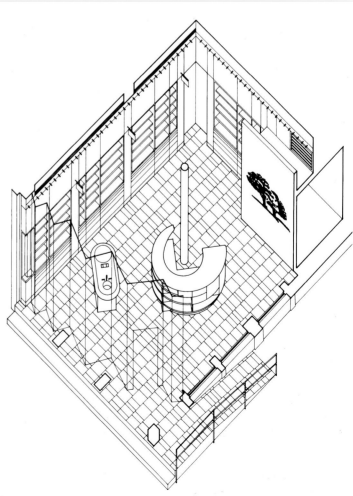

Ellen Tracy Boutique

THIRD FLOOR, BLOOMINGDALE'S
NEW YORK CITY

JAMES D'AURIA ASSOCIATES P.C. ARCHITECTS
NEW YORK CITY

This Ellen Tracy shop presents career-oriented bridge clothing by color, story, and delivery dates in bays anchored by pairs of black lacquer vitrines that serve as visual bookends. Grounded by an ivory travertine floor bordered in black granite, the concept is accentuated by furniture and freestanding fixtures.

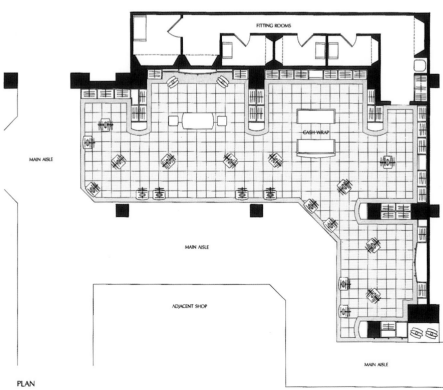

FITTING ROOMS

CASH WRAP

MAIN AISLE

MAIN AISLE

ADJACENT SHOP

MAIN AISLE

PLAN

FIRST PLACE

Aca Joe

PERISUR MALL, MEXICO CITY

Design
SPACE DESIGN INTERNATIONAL
CINCINNATI, OH

To change consumer perception from beachwear/T-shirt resource to an urban men's sportswear store anchored by jeans, the new design is influenced by English haberdashery. SDI redirected this look more toward young men and sportswear giving it Shaker-style fixtures and maple and Mexican tile flooring.

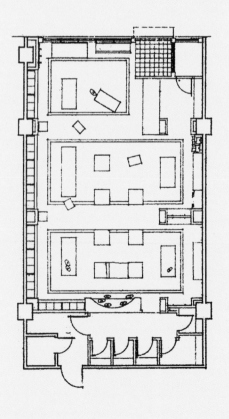

HONORABLE MENTION

Dockers Shop

CAMBRIDGE SIDE GALLERIA
CAMBRIDGE, MA

Design
BERGMEYER ASSOCIATES, INC.
BOSTON

A nautical theme and vacation vignettes recall soothing images of days on holiday for this store for Levi's Dockers apparel. Merchandise backdrops of wicker furniture and sailing complement angled, V-grooved panels stenciled with the Dockers logo, cherry soffits, and backlit art glass and props.

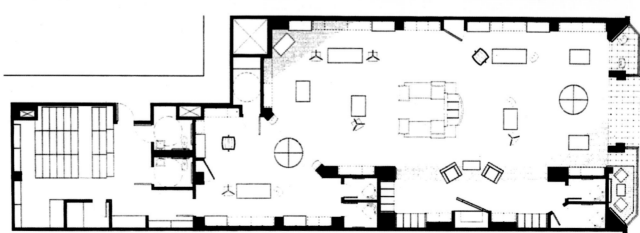

HONORABLE MENTION

Wolford Boutique

MADISON AVENUE, NEW YORK CITY

Design
JAMES D'AURIA ASSOCIATES
P.C. ARCHITECTS, NEW YORK CITY

To transform an awkwardly long and narrow space into an intimate selling environment for this colorful collection of hosiery and body-wear, the designers organized the space into a foyer with cashwrap, followed by hosiery and bodywear shops presenting the line's many colors, patterns, and textures.

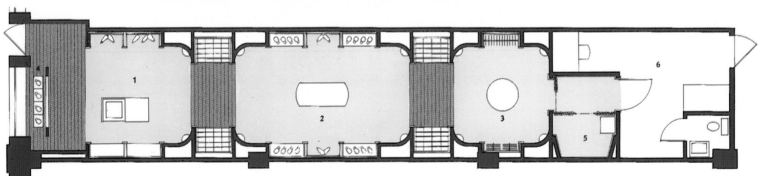

Windsor Fashions

DEL AMO FASHION CENTER
LOS ANGELES

Design
CHAIX & JOHNSON, INC.
LOS ANGELES

Chaix & Johnson's new design highlights each of Windsor's three businesses — career, casual, and special occasion apparel — and features service zones for each. The storefront's 13 1/2-foot windows and floating, sculptural sign of burnished copper and steel help de-emphasize the threshold.

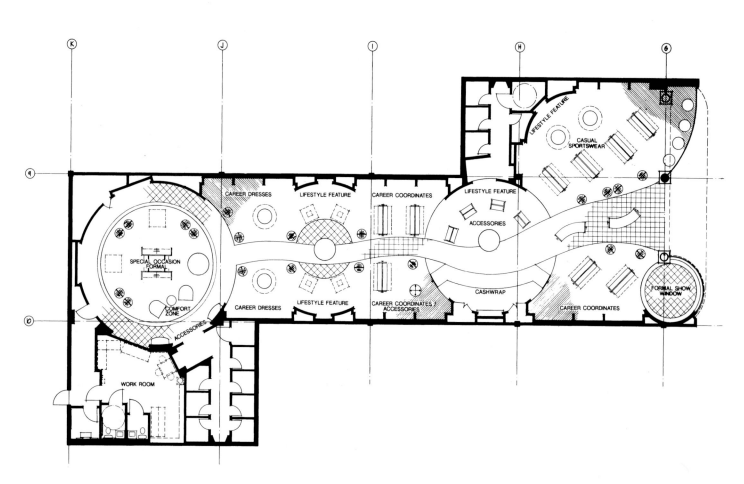

HONORABLE MENTION

Liz Claiborne

SOMERSET COLLECTION
TROY, MI

Design
HTI/SPACE DESIGN INTERNATIONAL
NEW YORK CITY

The new 8,400-square-foot Liz Claiborne prototype segments the vendor's entire line segmented by partial walls. Ivory and cream colors, natural light oak fixtures and flooring, sponge-painted walls, and silk tussah walls meet Liz's signature colors in aniline-dyed wood.

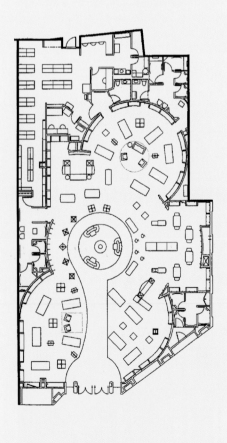

PETITES

FIRST PLACE

Steuben at the Greenbrier

THE GREENBRIER RESORT
WHITE SULPHER SPRINGS, WV

Design
LEE STOUT, INC., NEW YORK CITY

The Steuben Glass store at the historic resort hotel is sophisticated yet relaxed enough to welcome those clothed casually for golf and leisure. Virtually every light in the space is directed onto the glass, and most ambient illumination is a result of reflections and refractions from the light beams hitting the glass objects.

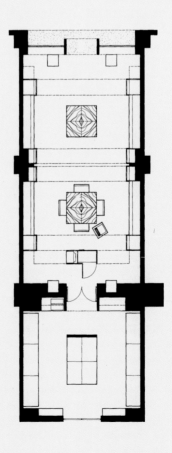

HONORABLE MENTION

Detroit Institute of Arts Museum Shop

SOMERSET COLLECTION
TROY, MI

Design
JON GREENBERG & ASSOCIATES, INC.
SOUTHFIELD, MI

Recreating the authenticity of the Detroit Institute of Arts' architectural heritage and rich cultural imagery, the 1,800-square-foot museum shop design is separated into "indoor" and "outdoor" areas. Art pieces and historical references abound.

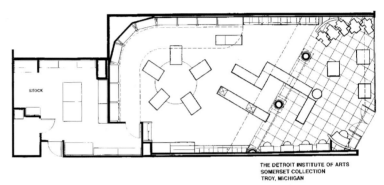

THE DETROIT INSTITUTE OF ARTS
SOMERSET COLLECTION
TROY, MICHIGAN

HONORABLE MENTION

Hall of Fame Sports Store

INNOVATION AWARD

FANEUIL HALL MARKETPLACE
BOSTON

Design
BERGMEYER ASSOCIATES, INC./
ROBERT M. WOOD ARCHITECTS, INC.
BOSTON

A part-store, part-museum format includes a varied display of licensed team apparel, sports collectibles, historic photography, and memorabilia set off by materials in deep green, oak, cherry, and maple. Garnering the Innovation honor was a central wall comprised of a series of display cases that hang asymmetrically from clustered, sand-blasted steel supports.

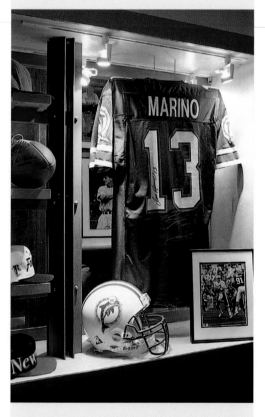

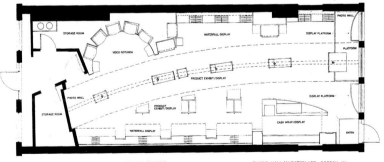

HALL OF FAME SPORTS   FANEUIL HALL MARKETPLACE BOSTON, MA

FIRST PLACE

Incredible Universe

TOWN CENTER LOOP WEST
WILSONVILLE, OR

Design
DESIGN FORUM, DAYTON, OH

Taking the category "killer approach" to a new level, Incredible Universe covers a total of 160,000 square feet of combined selling and warehouse space for consumer electronics. A host of shops are tied together with vibrant splashes of color, bright neon lights, and oversized signage and graphics perhaps best described as animated neon sculptures of the products within each department.

HONORABLE MENTION

Spectrum Music Superstore

LYONS CROSSING SHOPPING CENTER
MIAMISBURG, OH

Design
THE CHUTE GERDEMAN GROUP
COLUMBUS, OH

Intended as a seg-
mented entertainment superstore without walls and circulation barriers, the
multilevel Spectrum superstore came to
life in soffits with illuminated, full-color
graphics, a perimeter wall relief of
shapes, forms, and symbols, and indi-
rect light sources with colored gels for
each department.

HONORABLE MENTION

Toy Works

MALL OF AMERICA
BLOOMINGTON, MN

MELVILLE DESIGN CORP., RYE, NY

Toy Works customers can take in a broad vista of the store's vast interior via full-height glass windows. Throughout the store, the Toy Works logo, an architectural log and wheel, and fun geometric shapes adorn surfaces and complement simple gondolas, shelving, exposed ceilings, and a vinyl racetrack floor.

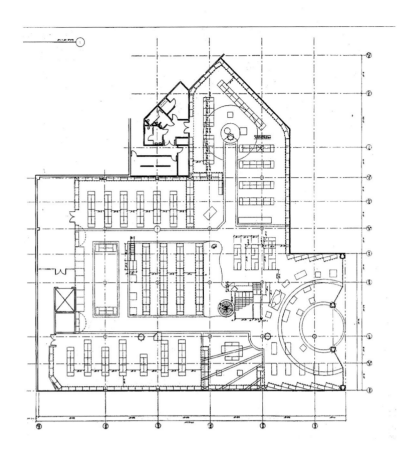

FIRST PLACE

New World Coffee

THIRD AVENUE, NEW YORK CITY

Design
RONNETTE RILEY ARCHITECT
NEW YORK CITY

New World Coffee is an attempt to evoke the warmth of experience and aroma associated with authentic espresso beverages. Naturally, earthy, coffee tones, stone, and wood come into play, as do a green-gold back-drop contrasted by cream-colored walls and floor. Lighting and a sharply angled counter punctuated by pendant lights along its edge draw the eye into the store from the streetfront.

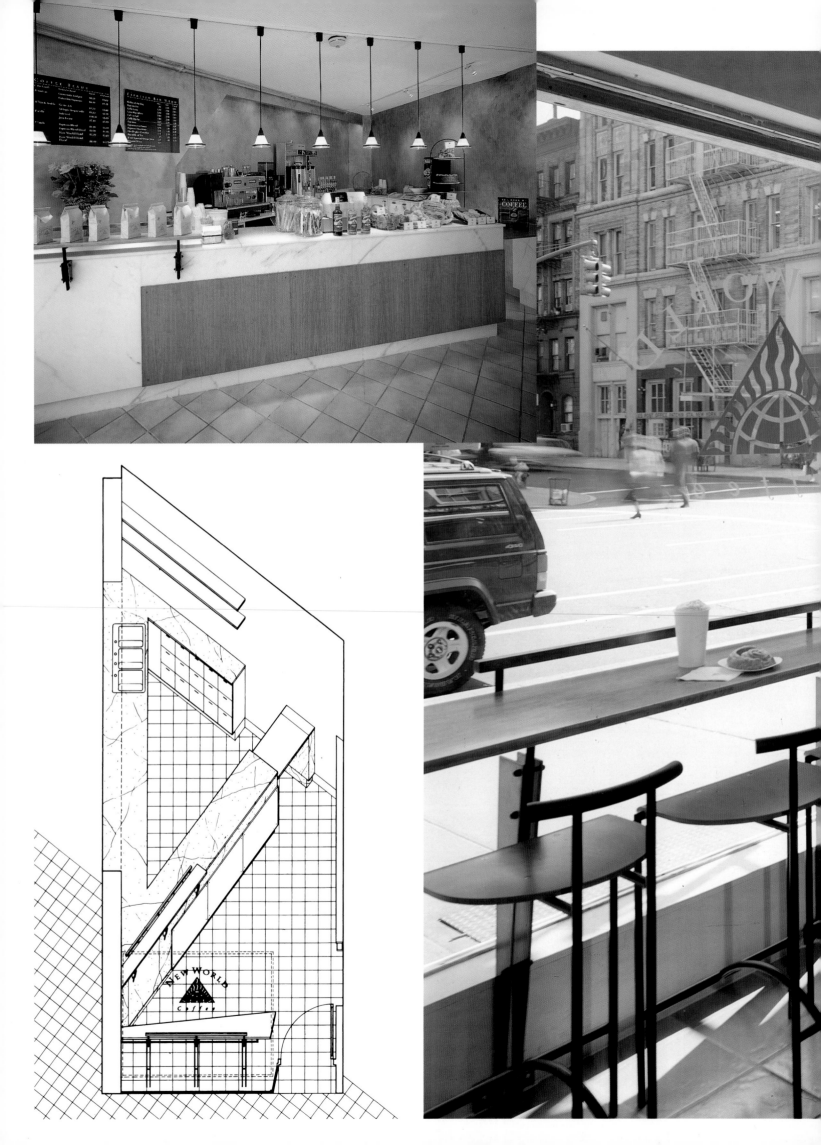

COFFEE BEANS

Coffee Family	Varietal or Blend	Pound	1/2 Pound
Americas	Guatemala Antigua	$8.19	$4.09
	Colombia Supremo	$6.49	$3.25
Africa & Arabia	Kenya AA	$7.79	$3.89
	Ethiopia Yergacheffe	$9.49	$4.75
Pacific	Sulawesi	$10.90	$5.49
	Java Estate	$7.39	$3.69
Blends	Espresso Blend	$8.19	$4.09
	Espresso Blend Decaf	$9.29	$4.6
	World Blend	$7.39	
	World Blend	$8.49	$4.25

LCBO Mini Store

FIRST CANADIAN PLACE, TORONTO

Design
INTERNATIONAL DESIGN GROUP
TORONTO

Searching for a new mini-store image with an up-market, fast-track approach, LCBO, the Liquor Control Board of Ontario, arrived at an arcade effect to help customers orient themselves quickly. The design includes decorative arches of bright copper tubes, geometric patterned flooring, and marble-clad columns.

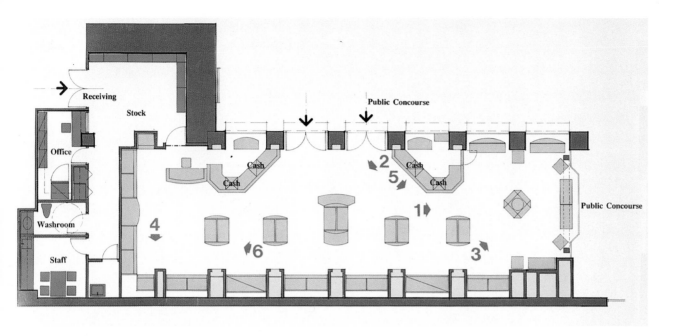

Penrith Plaza
Food Hall

PENRITH PLAZA, PENRITH, AUSTRALIA

Design
MARY BRANDON BY DESIGN
PYRMONT, AUSTRALIA

The fresh food market within the newly opened Plaza recreates the ambiance of country markets by incorporating individual stalls traditionally seen in Australia. A steel and timber grid overhead handles lighting, signage, and graphics.

Woolworth's
South Africa

FOURWAYS MALL
JOHANNESBURG, SOUTH AFRICA

Design
THE CHUTE GERDEMAN GROUP
COLUMBUS, OHIO

The two-level design for Woolworth's incorporates a barrel-vaulted ceiling and escalators in a fan formation. The classic simplicity of the Woolworth's logo and the "W" at the store entrance dictate the clean lines of the overall store design.

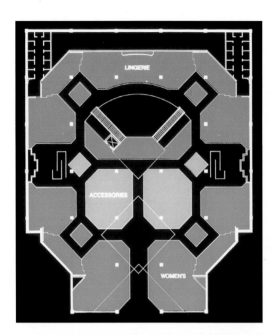

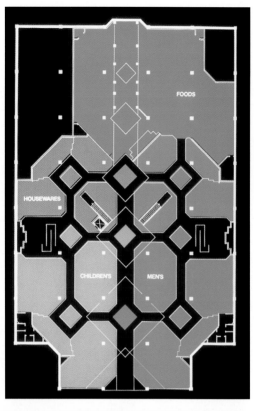

HONORABLE MENTION

Gran Bazar

PLAZA TOLUCA, TOLUCA, MEXICO

Design
SCHAFER ASSOCIATES, INC.
OAKBROOK TERRACE, IL

A 240,000-square-foot, one-level space large enough to fit four football fields, Gran Bazar features over 50 cashwraps, 2,000 shopping carts, and employee runners on roller skates. To organize the huge space into an easy-to-shop, fun environment took a color-coded plan of three merchandise worlds, strong graphics, and a flexible fixturing system to handle product that sometimes turns over within a few hours.

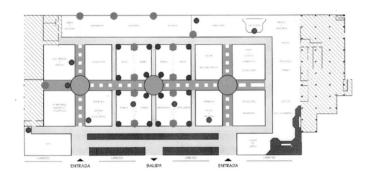

Outlet Marketplace

CASTLE ROCK FACTORY SHOPS
CASTLE ROCK, CO

Design
FITCH INC., WORTHINGTON, OH

A central "plaza and crossroads" orientation unifies this bazaar theme, while a hierarchical brand layout guides customers through the varied categories of the Marketplace. From here, an architectural threshold introduces each of the three major apparel classifications — casual, kids', and intimates.

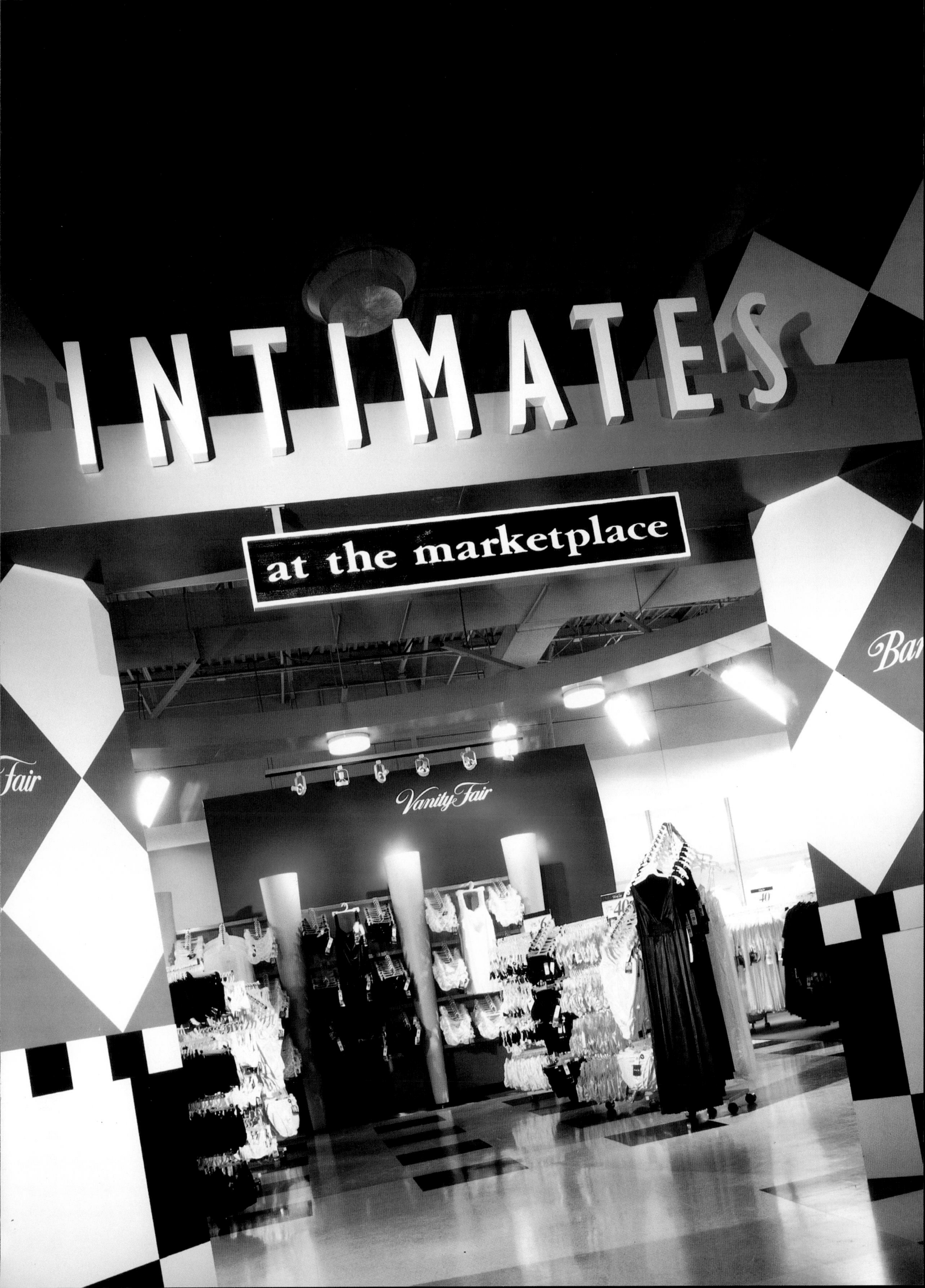
INTIMATES
at the marketplace
Vanity Fair

HONORABLE MENTION

Linens 'n Things

EASTGATE SQUARE
MT. LAUREL, NJ

Design
MELVILLE CORP., RYE, NY

Melville chose a racetrack configuration that combines ease of movement and continuity with the ability to create specific departments for merchandise categories. A specially designed, modular shelving system handles different stories and recedes to give the merchandise top billing.

HONORABLE MENTION

Marshall's

LIBERTY TREE MALL
DANVERS, MA

Design
JON GREENBERG & ASSOCIATES, INC.
SOUTHFIELD, MI

Striking a balance between Marshall's traditional off-price atmosphere and elements not usually found in a off-price environment, the remodeled Danvers Marshall's combines hard and soft materials, cold and warm color, and industrial-looking fixtures with flashes of "Marshall's Blue."

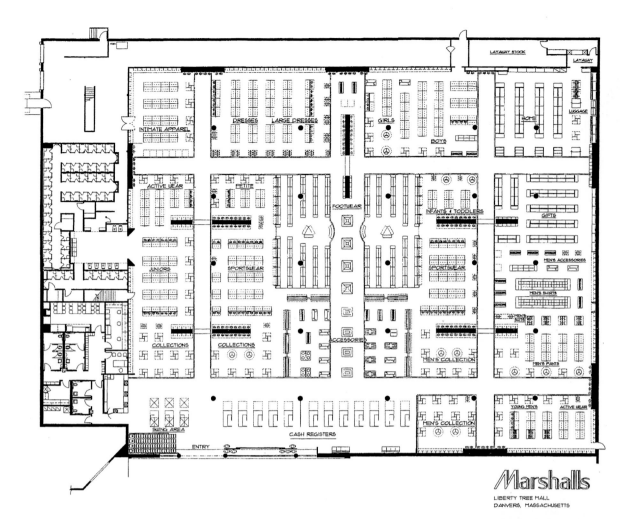

INTIMATE APPAREL

DRESSES   LARGE DRESSES

GIRLS

BOYS

HOME   LUGGAGE

ACTIVE WEAR

PETITE

FOOTWEAR

INFANTS & TODDLERS

GIFTS

JUNIORS

SPORTSWEAR

SPORTSWEAR

MEN'S ACCESSORIES

MEN'S SHIRTS

WOMEN'S SUITS

COLLECTIONS

COLLECTIONS

ACCESSORIES

MEN'S COLLECTION

MEN'S PANTS

SWING AREA

CASH REGISTERS

ENTRY

MEN'S COLLECTION

YOUNG MEN'S   ACTIVE WEAR

Marshalls

LIBERTY TREE MALL
DANVERS, MASSACHUSETTS

"My kids go through a lot of these. I need Marshalls!"

Shoes

Accessories

9.99

8-1/2   8-1/2

Kids   Kids
6   6

9.99   17.99

FIRST PLACE

Premier Bank

PLACE SAINT CHARLES
NEW ORLEANS

Design
FITCH INC., WORTHINGTON, OH

Premier Bank's environment is designed to communicate its "relationship building" strategy through an upbeat, comfortable consultative (rather than financial) setting. Dominant features include a spine that runs through the main space, boldly patterned carpet incorporating abstract New Orleans imagery, and an ATM cylinder intersecting the glass facade of the building.

HONORABLE MENTION

Cruise Holidays

INNOVATION AWARD

MALL OF AMERICA
BLOOMINGTON, MN

Design
WHEELER HILDEBRANDT &
ASSOCIATES, INC., MINNEAPOLIS, MN

Playing on the tropical fantasies of Minnesotans trapped in a blustery winter, the designers created a 700-square-foot retail oasis that gives shoppers at the Mall of America the feel of an exotic cruise voyage. Portholes peek in on sandy-beach carpeting, wave-like ceiling, and acrylic, sea-green dividers, deck chairs, beach umbrellas, and an overscaled smoke stack and a boat-shaped service station.

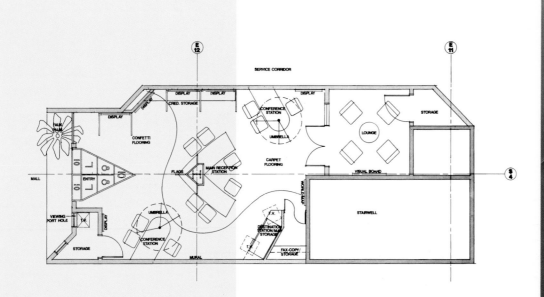

HONORABLE MENTION

The Monogram Shop

WESTFIELDS SHOPPINGTOWN
SYDNEY, AUSTRALIA

Design
DESIGN MOVEMENT
SYDNEY, AUSTRALIA

Located in a high vaulted, sunshine-filled food court, The Monogram Shop requires only minimum display space but maximum storage for customer gifts awaiting monogramming or pick-up. Two high-tech trussed towers, curved beams, and tensile rods secure dense canvas fabric as a sun screen and a free-form, curved counter increases the countertop space.

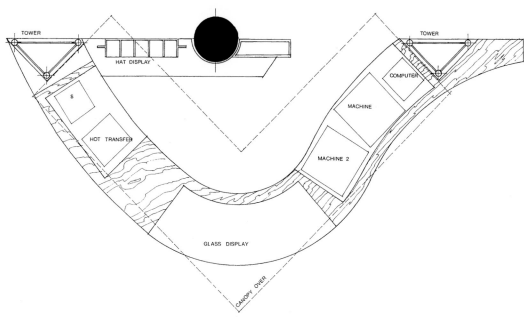

TOWER   TOWER

HAT DISPLAY

                                                    COMPUTER

            S   MACHINE

    HOT TRANSFER

                                    MACHINE 2

            GLASS DISPLAY

                    CANOPY OVER

FIRST PLACE

Six Flags Over Mid-America

INTERSTATE 44 AND ALLENTON,
EUREKA, MO

Design
JOHN ROBERTS & ASSOCIATES
SAN FRANCISCO

Asked to create a single store within a row of seven Victorian-style buildings loosely based on the 1904 St. Louis World's Fair, the designers took advantage of the color-saturated landscapes found only in Warner Bros. "Looney Tunes" cartoons. Special designs include a balloon that seems to drop through the ceiling, Wile E. Coyote's cave, a life-sized model of Sylvester the Cat's paw, and mahogany fixtures with a Victorian influence.

HONORABLE MENTION

KidsFun

NORTHCOURT, TAMPA, FL

Design
THE PAVLIK DESIGN TEAM
FT. LAUDERDALE, FL

Designed for kids 12 years and under and their parents, this play center kicks off with an illuminated, three-story kite-shaped entry arch and follows through on the fun theme with games, rides, bold colors and patterns, zigzag walls, undulating forms, and skewed aisles. A glass-enclosed parents's lounge is centrally located and offers maximum visibility along with peace and quiet.

Honorable Mention

Knott's Camp Snoopy Shops

Mall of America
Bloomington, MN

Design
International Design Group
New York City

These four of seven Camp Snoopy shops in the huge mall's indoor amusement park are based on the familiar neighborhood of Peanuts characters. Snoopy's doghouse features toys and clothing, while Woodstock's birdbath holds stuffed toys, Lucy Van Pelt sells T-shirts, and Peppermint Patty vends backpacks. Charlie Brown's lemonade stand is the cashwrap while Berry Market features Berry Farm gourmet items in a country kitchen setting.

1. SNOOPY'S BOUTIQUE

2. BERRY MARKET

4. CAMP SNOOPY TOYS

3. CRAFTS BARN

Knott's
BERRY FARM.
CAMP SNOOPY

92   INCREDIBLE UNIVERSE

TOWN CENTER LOOP WEST, WILSONVILLE, OR

DESIGN DESIGN FORUM, DAYTON, OH — SCOTT SMITH, SR. INDUSTRIAL DESIGN, PLANNER, DESIGNER AND JOB CAPTAIN; CAROLYN ZUDELL, CREATIVE DIRECTOR/GRAPHIC DESIGN; BRUCE DYBVAD, SENIOR VICE PRESIDENT DESIGN; D. LEE CARPENTER, CHAIRMAN AND CEO; **INCREDIBLE UNIVERSE DESIGN** RICH HOLLANDER; **CLIENT/OWNER** TANDY CORP., FORT WORTH, TEXAS; **ARCHITECT** DESIGN FORUM ARCHITECTS, DAYTON, OHIO; **SOUND CONSULTANT** RICHARD J. LIMKER & ASSOC., COVINGTON, KY.; **GENERAL CONTRACTOR** SD DEACON, PORTLAND, ORE.; **MILLWORK & FIXTURES** BUTLER GROUP, LOUISVILLE, KY.; **SIGNAGE** TANDY SIGN, ARLINGTON, TEXAS.

150   KIDSFUN

NORTHCOURT, TAMPA, FL

DESIGN THE PAVLIK DESIGN TEAM, FT. LAUDERDALE, FL— FERNANDO CASTILLO, PLANNER, DESIGNER, JOB CAPTAIN AND PROJECT CAPTAIN; PLACIDO HERRERA, DESIGNER, DECORATOR AND JOB CAPTAIN; ANGELA BUDANO, DESIGNER; LUIS VALLADARES, VICE PRESIDENT/PARTNER IN CHARGE; RONALD PAVLIK, PRESIDENT/CEO; **KIDSFUN DESIGN TEAM** ROBERT BOK, PLANNING; DIANE BOK, VISUAL MERCHANDISING; **CLIENT/OWNER** KIDSPLAY INC., BOCA RATON, FLA.; **ARCHITECT** JORGE HERNANDEZ ARCHITECT, HOLLYWOOD, FLA.; **GRAPHIC DESIGN AND LOGO** ANGELA BUDANO, THE PAVLIK DESIGN TEAM; **GENERAL CONTRACTOR** BEAUREGARD CONSTRUCTION INC., TAMPA, FLA.; **LIGHTING** LIGHTING DYNAMICS, INC., FT. LAUDERDALE, FLA.; **FURNITURE** ART EXTREMITIES, FT. LAUDERDALE, FLA. (CUSTOM THRONES AND BENCHES); FALCON PRODUCTS, FT. LAUDERDALE, FLA. (TABLES AND BASES); LOWENSTEIN, FT. LAUDERDALE, FLA. (CUSTOM CHAIRS); **SIGNAGE & GRAPHICS** INTERNATIONAL SIGN, TAMPA, FLA.; BANNER CREATIONS, MINNEAPOLIS; **PLAY EQUIPMENT** PLAYPAL INC., MERRIT ISLAND, FLA.; **FLOORING** ARMSTRONG, N. MIAMI BEACH, FLA.; KENTILE, MIAMI (VINYL); HARBINGER, POMPANO BEACH, FLA. (CARPET); SIKES TILE, FT. LAUDERDALE, FLA. (CERAMIC); DAL-TILE, FT. LAUDERDALE, FLA. (WALL TILE); **MATERIALS** FORMICA, CINCINNATI; WILSONART, TEMPLE, TEXAS (LAMINATES); BENJAMIN MOORE, MONTVALE, N.J., AND SHERWIN WILLIAMS, CLEVELAND (PAINT).

152   KNOTT'S CAMP SNOOPY SHOPS

MALL OF AMERICA, BLOOMINGTON, MN

DESIGN THE INTERNATIONAL DESIGN GROUP, NEW YORK CITY — KEITH KOVAR, PLANNER; RUTH MELLERGAARD, JOJO BORJA AND CHRISTINE CARDELLO, DESIGNERS; ERROL DEMAGAJES, JOB CAPTAIN; RUTH MELLERGAARD, VICE PRESIDENT/PARTNER IN CHARGE; **KNOTT'S CAMP SNOOPY DESIGN TEAM** KEN DONHAM, VISUAL MERCHANDISING; KAREN YOSHIKOWA, VICE PRESIDENT MERCHANDISING (YOSHIKAWA & ASSOCIATES, ORANGE, CALIF.); **CLIENT/OWNER** ROBIN HALL, BUENA PARK, CALIF.; **ARCHITECT** HOPE ARCHITECTS, SAN DIEGO; **GENERAL CONTRACTOR** MELVIN SIMON & ASSOCIATES, INDIANAPOLIS; **LIGHTING** HALO LIGHTING, ELK GROVE VILLAGE, ILL.; **FIXTURES** SPACEWALL INT'L., STONE MOUNTAIN, GA. (SLATWALL); GARCY CORP., MELROSE PARK, ILL. (STANDARDS); **MATERIALS** OLYMPIC, WAYNE, N.J. (WOOD FINISH); SHERWIN WILLIAMS, CLEVELAND (PAINT); FORMICA, CINCINNATI; WILSONART, TEMPLE, TEXAS (PLASTIC LAMINATE); SHIP 'N OUT, BREWSTER, N.Y. (METAL TRIM); ARMSTRONG WORLD INDUSTRIES, SADDLE BROOK, N.J. (CEILING TILE); SILVERTON VICTORIAN MILLWORK, DURANGO, COLO. (WOOD MOLDING).

56   LA PRAIRIE IN-STORE BOUTIQUE

BLOOMINGDALE'S, MAIN FLOOR, NEW YORK CITY

DESIGN NORWOOD OLIVER DESIGN ASSOCIATES, INC., NEW YORK CITY — ED ALLISON, PROJECT MANAGER; STEPHEN YOUNG, EXECUTIVE VICE PRESIDENT; KAREN WENZEL-MURPHY, VICE PRESIDENT DESIGN DIRECTOR; NORWOOD OLIVER, PRESIDENT/CEO; NODA'S STAFF, DESIGN, PLANNING AND DECORATING DEPARTMENTS; **GENERAL CONTRACTOR AND SUPPLIER** STEINGART WOODCRAFTERS INC., BROOKLYN, N.Y.

112   LCBO MINI STORE

FIRST CANADIAN PLACE, TORONTO

DESIGN THE INTERNATIONAL DESIGN GROUP, TORONTO — DAVID NEWMAN, PLANNER, DESIGNER, JOB CAPTAIN AND PROJECT MANAGER; RON MAZEREEUW AND JOHN SHAVER; RONALD HARRIS, PRESIDENT; **LCBO MINI STORE DESIGN TEAM** GLEN COOK, JACKIE BONIC, TAMARA BURNS; **CLIENT/OWNER** LIQUOR CONTROL BOARD OF ONTARIO (LCBO), TORONTO; **ARCHITECT** INTERNATIONAL DESIGN GROUP INC.; **LIGHTING CONSULTANT** JUNO LIGHTING, TORONTO; **GENERAL CONTRACTOR** SALWOOD GENERAL CONTRACTORS, TORONTO; **MILLWORK** SALWOOD GENERAL CONTRACTORS; **FLOORING** CIOT & FERLEO.

128   LINENS 'N THINGS

EASTGATE SQUARE, MT. LAUREL, NJ

DESIGN MELVILLE CORP., RYE, NY — IN-HOUSE CONSTRUCTION, DESIGN & STORE PLANNING GROUPS; **LINENS 'N THINGS DESIGN TEAM** IN-HOUSE STORE MERCHANDISING GROUP; **ARCHITECT** THE TRICARICO GROUP, TOTOWA, N.J.; **GENERAL CONTRACTOR** VESTERRA GROUP, SHIPACK, PA.; **LIGHTING** SLP, WOODBRIDGE, N.J.; CAPITOL LIGHT & SUPPLY, HARTFORD, CONN.; **FIXTURES** ZELL BROTHERS, RED LION, PA.; **SIGNAGE** VISCO SIGN, NEW YORK CITY; MIDTOWN NEON SIGN, NEW YORK CITY; **FLOORING** J&J CARPETS, DALTON, GA. (CARPET).

82   LIZ CLAIBORNE

SOMERSET COLLECTION, TROY, MI

DESIGN HTI/SPACE DESIGN INTERNATIONAL, NEW YORK CITY — FRANCIS ASSAF, PLANNER AND PROJECT MANAGER; BRYAN GAILEY, DESIGNER; LESLIE LARM HARALSON, DECORATOR; ED HAMBRECHT, PARTNER IN CHARGE; JAMES FITZGERALD, PRESIDENT/CEO; ISRAEL GERBER, DIRECTOR OF COST CONTROL; **LIZ CLAIBORNE DESIGN TEAM** ALLEN MCNEARY, BRAD LENZ, WADE PETTY, RENEE VIOLA; **LIGHTING CONSULTANT** SASKIA KOK-TRICOMI, HTI/SDI; **CONSULTANTS** AVCON DESIGN GROUP, NEW YORK CITY (MECHANICAL/ELECTRICAL ENGINEERING); **GENERAL CONTRACTOR** TUCCI CONSTRUCTION, BROOKLYN, N.Y.; **LIGHTING** INDY LIGHTING, INDIANAPOLIS; **FLOORING** STRATTON, NEW YORK CITY (CARPET); COUNTRY FLOORS, NEW YORK CITY (CERAMIC TILING); STARK CARPET CORP., NEW YORK CITY, AND CYRUS CARPETS, NEW YORK CITY (AREA RUGS); **WALL COVERING** BILL CORRY, RIVERHEAD, N.Y.; **MATERIALS** EUROPEAN SURFACES, NEW YORK CITY (SPECIAL PAINT); LAUE INC., LONG ISLAND CITY, N.Y. (COLORED WOOD VENEER); WILSONART, TEMPLE, TEXAS (PLASTIC LAMINATE).

6   MARK SHALE

COUNTRY CLUB PLAZA, KANSAS CITY, MO

DESIGN CHARLES SPARKS + CO., WESTCHESTER, IL — CHARLES SPARKS, PLANNER, DESIGNER, VICE PRESIDENT/PARTNER IN CHARGE AND PRESIDENT/CEO; FRED WIEDENBECK, JIM HANSON AND RACHEL SCHEU, DECORATORS; MIKE SPARKS, JOB CAPTAIN, DON STONE, PROJECT MANAGER; **MARK SHALE DESIGN TEAM** SCOTT BASKIN, PRESIDENT; SHALE BASKIN, CHAIR; STEVE BASKIN, EXECUTIVE VICE PRESIDENT; JILL KURTH, VISUAL MERCHANDISE; **CLIENT/OWNER** MARK SHALE, WILLOWBROOK, ILL.; **ARCHITECT** MARK SPARKS, WESTCHESTER, ILL.; **CONSULTANT** KHATIB & ASSOCIATES, ENGINEERS, CHICAGO; **GENERAL CONTRACTOR** WINN-SENTER CONSTRUCTION, KANSAS CITY, MO.; **STAIRS** ZEPHYR METAL, TULSA, OKLA.; **MILLWORK & CABINETRY**; BERNHARD WOODWORK, NORTHBROOK, ILL. ; **WALL SYSTEM** COLUMBUS INDUSTRIES, COLUMBUS, OHIO; **LIGHTING** LIGHTOLIER, SECAUCUS, N.J.; DAY-O-LITE, WARWICK, R.I.; MORRISON CUSTOM LIGHTING, NOVATO, CALIF., AND BOYD LIGHTING, SAN FRANCISCO (LAMPS); **FURNITURE** THOS. MOSER CABINET MAKERS, AUBURNE, MAINE; BERNARDT CONTRACT, CHICAGO; KNOLL GROUP, CHICAGO; FETZER'S, SALT LAKE CITY; **ARTWORK** MODE WORKS, NEW YORK CITY (CUSTOM FINE ART); BRAD BASKIN, CHICAGO (FRAMED PHOTOGRAPHY); **FLOORING** BENTLEY MILLS, CHICAGO (CARPET & AREA RUGS); DAL-TILE, ELK GROVE, ILL. (SLATE); BRANN CLAY PRODUCTS, ALSIP, ILL. (CERAMIC); **WALL COVERINGS** BLUMENTHAL, LONG ISLAND CITY, N.Y.; MAYA ROMANOFF, CHICAGO; SOUDART DESIGN, EDGEWATER, N.J.; SILK DYNASTY, MOUNTAIN VIEW, CALIF; FORBO-VICRTEX, INC., HAZELTON, PA.; SLOAN DAVIS, OAK PARK, ILL.; **MATERIALS** BENJAMIN MOORE, MONTVALE, N.J., AND ZOLATONE/MGA ASSOCIATES, CHICAGO (PAINT).

132   MARSHALL'S

LIBERTY TREE MALL, DANVERS, MA

DESIGN JON GREENBERG & ASSOCIATES, INC., SOUTHFIELD, MI — MICHAEL MCCAHILL AND SUSAN MORGOWICZ, PLANNERS; SUSAN HAIFLEIGH, DESIGNER; MICHELE MARTINES, DECORATOR; ED DURANT, PROJECT MANAGER; KENNETH NISCH, PRESIDENT/CEO; **MARSHALL'S DESIGN** MARK BRAUN; **CLIENT/OWNER** WARREN FELDBERG, ANDOVER, MASS.; **ARCHITECT** JON GREENBERG & ASSOCIATES; **CONSULTANT** ILLUMINATING CONCEPTS, FARMINGTON HILLS, MICH.; **GENERAL CONTRACTOR** ARNOLD PEDERSON BUILDING CORP., DEERFIELD, ILL.; **COLUMN COVERS** DEC ASSOCIATES, COMPTON, CALIF.; **CEILING** U.S.G., CHICAGO; **LIGHTING** DAYBRITE, TUPELO, MISS.; LIGHTRON, NEW WINDSOR, N.Y.; ZUMTOBEL, FAIRFIELD, N.J.; KRAMER, NEWPORT, KY.; CAPRI, LOS ANGELES; HALO, ELK GROVE VILLAGE, ILL.; **FIXTURES** GARCY CORP., MELROSE PARK, ILL.; **FURNITURE** KRUEGER INT'L., GREEN BAY, WIS.; **GRAPHICS** RAINBOW SIGNS, INC., BLOOMINGTON, MINN.; **FLOORING** FLOR-TEK CONSULTANTS, HULL, MASS. (EPOXY); MILLIKEN, LAGRANGE, GA. (CARPET); **WALL COVERING** FORBO-VICRTEX, INC., HAZELTON, PA.; **MATERIALS** BENJAMIN MOORE, MONTVALE, N.J., AND ZOLATONE, GLOUCESTER, MASS. (PAINT); NEVAMAR, ODENTON, MD., PIONITE, AUBURN, MAINE, AND WILSONART, TEMPLE, TEXAS (LAMINATES).

142   THE MONOGRAM SHOP

WESTFIELDS SHOPPINGTOWN, LIVERPOOL, AUSTRALIA

DESIGN DESIGN MOVEMENT, SYDNEY, AUSTRALIA — TOM COSGROVE; **CLIENT/OWNER** TED DUONG, LIVERPOOL, AUSTRALIA; **GENERAL CONTRACTOR** PAUL WINKLE CONTRACTORS, SYDNEY, AUSTRALIA; **LIGHTING** NEOZ P/L, SYDNEY, AUSTRALIA; OPTIMA, SYDNEY, AUSTRALIA; **MATERIALS** NEW AGE VENEERS, SYDNEY, AUSTRALIA (VENEERS).

108   NEW WORLD COFFEE

1159 THIRD AVENUE, NEW YORK CITY

DESIGN RONNETTE RILEY ARCHITECT, NEW YORK CITY — DALE LINDEN TURNER, PROJECT ARCHITECT; RONNETTE RILEY, PARTNER IN CHARGE; **ARCHITECT** RONNETTE RILEY ARCHITECT; **LIGHTING CONSULTANT** JOHNSON SCHWINGHAMMER, INC., NEW YORK CITY; **FOOD SERVICE CONSULTANT** POST & GROSSBARD, PIERMONT, N.Y.; **GENERAL CONTRACTOR AND CUSTOM CABINETRY** JOTA CONSTRUCTION, WOODBRIDGE, N.J.; **CONTRACTORS** AVCON DESIGN GROUP, NEW YORK CITY (MECHANICAL ENGINEER); **LIGHTING** LEUCOS USA INC., EDISON, N.J.; INDY LIGHTING INC., INDIANAPOLIS; **FURNITURE** GULLANS INT'L. INC., NEW YORK CITY (STOOLS); **GRAPHICS** RONNETTE RILEY ARCHITECT; REAL DESIGN, NEW YORK CITY; **SPECIAL FINISHES** PHILIPPANA CORP., NEW YORK CITY (PAINT); STUDIO AVIVI, NEW YORK CITY (ORNAMENTAL METAL); **FLOORING** QUARRY TILE, MONOCIBEC ASSISI, (CITY UNKNOWN).

60 ORIGINS

ORIGINS, WEST BROADWAY, NEW YORK CITY

DESIGN PETER FORBES & ASSOCIATES, BOSTON — PETER FORBES, PROJECT DESIGN, PLANNER AND DESIGNER; BRADFORD WALKER, PROJECT DESIGN, JOB CAPTAIN AND PROJECT MANAGER; WILLIAM RUHL, PROJECT DESIGN TEAM; MECHANICAL/PLUMBING/ELECTRICAL ENGINEER COSENTINI ASSOCIATES, CAMBRIDGE, MASS.; ARCHITECT PETER FORBES AND ASSOCIATES, BOSTON; SOUND ARTIST CHRISTOPHER JANNEY, BOSTON; GENERAL CONTRACTOR CLARK CONSTRUCTION, NEW YORK CITY; CONTRACTORS ANCHOR PLUMBING, BROOKLYN, N.Y.; ALBA ELECTRICAL, BROOKLYN, N.Y.; MILKEY, LONG ISLAND CITY, N.Y. (PAINTING); LIGHTING ALBA ELECTRICAL, BROOKLYN, N.Y.; MILLWORK C.W. KELLER & ASSOCIATES, INC., PLAISTOW, N.H.; C.W. KELLER, PLAISTOW, N.H. (ARCHITECTURAL WOODWORK); FURNITURE PETER FORBES AND ASSOCIATES, BOSTON; SIGNAGE GILBEY GRAPHICS, NEW YORK CITY; HAND FABRICATIONS, NEW YORK CITY; POINT-OF-SALE & PRODUCT TESTER MERCHANDISING UNITS P.O.P. DISPLAY, LONG ISLAND CITY, N.Y.; MATERIALS PORT MORRIS, PATERSON, N.J. (STONE); LANCER METALS, ASTORIA, N.Y. (STOREFRONT AND GLASS); HAND FABRICATIONS, NEW YORK CITY (ARCHITECTURAL METALS).

124 VF OUTLET MARKETPLACE

CASTLE ROCK FACTORY SHOPS, CASTLE ROCK, CO

DESIGN FITCH INC., WORTHINGTON, OH — BETH DORSEY, PROJECT MANAGER, VICE PRESIDENT; ALYCIA FREEMAN, MARIBETH GATCHALIAN, KELLY MOONEY, ELLEN HARTSHORNE AND PAUL HARLOR, DESIGNERS; MARTIN BECK, CEO; CLIENT/OWNER VF FACTORY OUTLET, READING, PA.; ARCHITECT TERRY LEE & ASSOCIATES, TUSCON, ARIZ.; CONSULTANT LIGHTING MANAGEMENT, NEW YORK CITY; GENERAL CONTRACTOR VF CORP., READING, PA.; FLOORING AZROCK TILE, SAN ANTONIO (VCT); EUROTEX, PHILADELPHIA (CARPET); MATERIALS SHERWIN WILLIAMS, CLEVELAND (PAINT); NEVAMAR, ODENTON, MD., AND ABET LAMINATI, TETERBORO, N.J. (PLASTIC LAMINATE); DAYTON PLASTICS, DAYTON, OHIO (PLASTICS).

20 PARISIAN

TOWN CENTER MALL, KENNESAW, GA.

DESIGN WALKERGROUP/CNI, NEW YORK CITY — DAVID WALES, DESIGNER; STEVE KITEZH AND STEVE ICKERT, DECORATORS; MAURICIO GONZALEZ, JOB CAPTAIN; DAVID MCQUILKEN, PROJECT MANAGER; ROBERT CARULLO, VICE PRESIDENT/PARTNER IN CHARGE; MARK PUCCI, PRESIDENT/CEO; PARISIAN DESIGN TEAM CRAIG CAMPBELL, PRINCIPAL; JIM MITCHELL, DIRECTOR; BILL MCREYNOLDS, PROJECT MANAGER ; ARCHITECT CRAWFORD, MCWILLIAMS & HATCHER, BIRMINGHAM, ALA.; LIGHTING CONSULTANT JOHN SCHWINGHAMMER, NEW YORK CITY; GENERAL CONTRACTOR BRASFIELD & GORRIE, BIRMINGHAM, ALA.; CONTRACTORS ALAN PAINTING AND DECORATING, NEW YORK CITY; MILLWORK T.J. HALE CO., MENOMONEE FALLS, WIS.; DMS STORE FIXTURES, KING OF PRUSSIA, PA.; BUILDERS FURNITURE LTD., WINNIPEG, MAN.; SPECIAL FIXTURES GEORGE DELL, NEW YORK CITY; FURNITURE HBF, HICKORY, N.C.; CARTWRIGHT, HIGHPOINT, N.C.; BERNHARDT, LENOIR, N.C.; LOWENSTEIN, POMPANO BEACH, FLA.; BONAVENTURE, MONTREAL; CARL KISABETH CO. INC., FORT WORTH, TEXAS; SANDER PARTNERSHIP, LONG ISLAND CITY, N.Y.; GIE INT'L., LONG ISLAND CITY, N.Y.; FLOORING DURKAN CARPETS, DALTON, GA.; PRINCE STREET TECHNOLOGIES (CARPET), ATLANTA; J.C. ODUM (TERRAZZO), MONROE, GA.; INNOVATIVE MARBLE AND TILE, FARMINGDALE, N.Y.; CATCO MARBLE, E. BRUNSWICK, N.J.; WALL COVERINGS CHIAROSCURO, NEW YORK CITY; MAYA ROMANOFF, CHICAGO; TANDEM CONTRACT INC., MONMOUTH JUNCTION, N.J.; LAUE WALLCOVERING INC., LONG ISLAND CITY, N.Y.; DESIGNTEX, WOODSIDE, N.Y.; WILLOW TEXTILES, LONG ISLAND CITY, N.Y.; MATERIALS BENJAMIN MOORE, MONTVALE, N.J. (PAINT); DUPONT, WILMINGTON, DEL. (SPECIAL FINISHES); ABET LAMINATI, TETERBORO, N.J.; FORMICA, CINCINNATI (LAMINATES); DESIGNTEX, WOODSIDE, N.Y. (UPHOLSTERY FABRICS).

114 PENRITH PLAZA FOOD HALL

PENRITH PLAZA, PENRITH, AUSTRALIA

DESIGN MARY BRANDON BY DESIGN, PYRMONT, AUSTRALIA — MARY BRANDON, PLANNER, DESIGNER, VICE PRESIDENT/PARTNER IN CHARGE AND PRESIDENT/CEO; MICHELLE TAYLOR, TENANCY CRITIQUE DESIGNER; FENG ZHAN, DESIGNER; CIVIL & CIVIC, SYDNEY, AUSTRALIA, PROJECT MANAGER; PENRITH PLAZA FOOD HALL DESIGN TEAM LEND LEASE RETAIL GROUP, SYDNEY, AUSTRALIA; LEND LEASE DESIGN GROUP, SYDNEY, AUSTRALIA; CLIENT/OWNER ANZ BANK/GENERAL PROPERTY TRUST, SYDNEY, AUSTRALIA; ARCHITECT LEND LEASE DESIGN GROUP, SYDNEY, AUSTRALIA; GRAPHICS CONSULTANT ANNETTE HARCUS DESIGN, SYDNEY, AUSTRALIA; LIGHTING CONSULTANT T. KONDOS & ASSOCIATES, NEW YORK CITY; GENERAL CONTRACTOR CIVIL & CIVIC, SYDNEY, AUSTRALIA; CEILING HUNTER DOUGLAS, DULUTH, GA.; FURNITURE STREET FURNITURE, SYDNEY, AUSTRALIA.

136 PREMIER BANK

PLACE SAINT CHARLES, NEW ORLEANS

DESIGN FITCH INC., WORTHINGTON, OH — DAN DORSEY, PROJECT MANAGER; P. KELLY MOONEY AND PAUL LECHLEITER, DESIGNERS; MARTIN BECK, CEO; PREMIER BANK DESIGN BIFF MOTLEY, EXECUTIVE VICE PRESIDENT; PROJECT ARCHITECT SIZELER ARCHITECTS, NEW ORLEANS; LIGHTING FLOS INC., HUNTINGTON STATION, N.Y.; FURNITURE STEELCASE, GRAND RAPIDS, MICH.; FLOORING CHRISTOPHER GUARISCO, NEW ORLEANS (CARPET); WALL COVERING DUROPLEX, HOUSTON; PIONEER PLASTICS CORP., AUBURN, MAINE; FORMICA CORP., CINCINNATI; MATERIALS DONGHIA, NEW YORK CITY (LOBBY CHAIRS FABRIC).

14 RICH'S

NORTHPOINT MALL, ATLANTA, GA

DESIGN HTI/SPACE DESIGN INTERNATIONAL, NEW YORK CITY — JAYNE PETERSON, PLANNER; BRYAN GAILEY, DESIGN PRINCIPAL; MARK FENTON, DESIGNER; DEBRA ROBUSTO, DECORATOR; DICK MIKULSKI, JOB CAPTAIN; MIKE GNECCO, PROJECT MANAGER; JOHN CZORNY, VICE PRESIDENT/PARTNER IN CHARGE; JAMES FITZGERALD, PRESIDENT/CEO; SASKIA KOK-TRICOMI, LIGHTING DESIGNER; ISRAEL GERBER, DIRECTOR OF COST CONTROL; RICH'S DESIGN TEAM DAVID WIDMER, VICE PRESIDENT VISUAL MERCHANDISING; JEFF MATHEWS, VICE PRESIDENT STORE PLANNING; GREG BAKER, CONSTRUCTION MANAGER; PAUL REEDER, FEDERATED TEAM; CLIENT/OWNER FEDERATED DEPARTMENT STORES, CINCINNATI; ARCHITECT COOPER CAREY & ASSOCIATES, ATLANTA; GENERAL CONTRACTOR WINTER CONSTRUCTION, ATLANTA; LIGHTING LIGHTOLIER, SECAUCUS, N.J.; INDY LIGHTING, INDIANAPOLIS; SPI LIGHTING, MEQUON, WIS.; STAFF LIGHTING, HIGHLAND, N.Y.; FIXTURES RON HENDERSON ASSOCIATES, MEMPHIS, TENN.; MERCHANDISE EQUIPMENT INC., ATLANTA; GOEBBEL, HUTCHINSON, MINN.; FURNITURE BARRETT HILL, NEW YORK CITY; SWAIM, HIGH POINT, N.C.; RIALTO, BROOKLYN, N.Y.; SHELBY WILLIAMS, MORRISTOWN, TENN.; FLOORING INNOVATIVE MARBLE & TILE, HAUPPAUGE, N.Y. (MARBLE); PERMAGRAIN, MEDIA, PA., AND THE APPLIED RADIANT ENERGY CORP., FOREST, VA. (WOOD); ATLAS CARPET, LOS ANGELES, MOHAWK, ATLANTA, AND DURKAN, DALTON, GA. (CARPET); WALL COVERINGS SILK DYNASTY, MOUNTAIN VIEW, CALIF.; DESIGNTEX, WOODSIDE, N.Y.; WOLF GORDON, LONG ISLAND CITY, N.Y.; J.M. LYNNE, SMITHTOWN, N.Y.; ART PEOPLE, NEW YORK CITY; LAUE INC., LONG ISLAND CITY, N.Y.; MAYA ROMANOFF, CHICAGO; MATERIALS BENJAMIN MOORE, MONTVALE, N.J., AND SPECIALTY PAINT, ATLANTA (PAINT).

16 SALINAS Y ROCHA

LA GRAN PLAZA, ACAPULCO, MEXICO

DESIGN SCHAFER ASSOCIATES, INC., OAKBROOK TERRACE, IL — ROBERT SCHAFER, PLANNER, PRESIDENT/CEO; STEVE PROSSER, DESIGNER; JOSEPH DRENDEL, JOB CAPTAIN; SALINAS Y ROCHA DESIGN GUSTAVO QUINTANA, ING.; GENERAL CONTRACTOR SATME, S.A. DE C.V.; FLOORING BENTLEY MILLS, CITY OF INDUSTRY, CALIF. (CARPET); MATERIALS FORMICA, CINCINNATI, AND WILSONART, TEMPLE, TEXAS (LAMINATES); SHERWIN WILLIAMS, CLEVELAND, AND MULTICOLOR SPECIALTIES, CICERO, ILL., (PAINT).

26 SAKS FIFTH AVENUE

611 FIFTH AVENUE, SIXTH FLOOR MEN'S DEPARTMENT, NEW YORK CITY

DESIGN FITZPATRICK DESIGN GROUP, INC., NEW YORK CITY — GERALD BRIENZA, PLANNER AND VICE PRESIDENT/PARTNER IN CHARGE; ANDREW MCQUILKIN, DESIGNER; LISA BENSON, DECORATOR; CHARLES ARATO, PROJECT MANAGER; JAY FITZPATRICK, CREATIVE DIRECTOR; SAKS FIFTH AVENUE DESIGN TEAM FRANK KELLAR, VICE PRESIDENT OF STORE PLANNING & DESIGN; GIRARD SAKEE, STORE PLANNER; LIGHTING CONSULTANT JOHN SCIACCA/MERCHANDISE LIGHTING INC., PORT JERVIS, N.Y.; FIXTURES CRAFTED CABINETS, BRONX, N.Y.; T.J. HALE, MENOMONEE FALLS, WIS.; FURNITURE BFC/BFI, NEW YORK CITY; CARTWRIGHT C/O LEVINE CALVANO ASSOCIATES, LONG ISLAND CITY, N.Y.; CHAIRMASTERS, BRONX, N.Y.; DESIGN AMERICA/SPINNYBECK, NEW YORK CITY; DESIGN INSTITUTE OF AMERICA, NEW YORK CITY; ESCART INT'L./PUCCI INT'L., NEW YORK CITY; FELDMAN BROTHERS, LONG ISLAND CITY, N.Y.; HICKORY BUSINESS FURNITURE/CN ASSOCIATES, LONG ISLAND CITY, N.Y.; INTERIOR CRAFT, CHICAGO; JOEL NORMAN, NEW YORK CITY; MANHEIM GALLERIES, DALLAS; NIEDERMAIER INC. C/O SILVER ASSOCIATES, NEW YORK CITY; SHELBY WILLIAMS, NEW YORK CITY; UPHOLSTERY JACK LENOR LARSEN, NEW YORK CITY, AND SANDER PARTNERSHIP, LONG ISLAND CITY, N.Y.; FLOORING BENTLEY MILLS, NEW YORK CITY, CARPET INNOVATIONS, INC., NEW YORK CITY, DURKAN CARPETS/COMTECH, NEW YORK CITY, KARASTAN BIGELOW, NEW YORK CITY, AND PATERSON, FLYNN, MARTIN & MANGES, NEW YORK CITY (CARPET); INNOVATIVE MARBLE & TILE, HAUPPAUGE, N.Y. (MARBLE); W.D. VIRTURE CO., SUMMIT, N.J. (CERAMIC TILE); ARMSTRONG FLOORING, LANCASTER, PA. (VINYL BASE); AZROCK, RUTHERFORD, N.J. (VINYL TILE); HOBOKEN WOOD FLOORS, WAYNE, N.J. (WOOD); WALL COVERING CARNEGIE FABRICS, NEW YORK CITY; DEEPA FABRICS, LONG ISLAND CITY, N.Y.; DESIGN TEX, NEW YORK CITY; JACK LENOR LARSEN, NEW YORK CITY; KRAVET FABRICS, NEW YORK CITY; ROBERT ALLEN FABRICS, NEW YORK CITY; WILLOW TEX, LONG ISLAND CITY, N.Y.; ZIMMERMAN & RHODE C/O JACK LENOR LARSEN, NEW YORK CITY; MATERIALS DEEPA FABRICS, LONG ISLAND CITY, N.Y., KRAVET FABRICS, NEW YORK CITY, AND ZIMMERMAN & RHODE C/O JACK LENOR LARSEN, NEW YORK CITY (FABRIC); MILGO BUFKIN, BROOKLYN, N.Y. (METAL); DAVID R. WEBB, TENAFLY, N.J., AND VENEER PRODUCTS LTD., LONG ISLAND CITY, N.Y. (NATURAL FINISH WOOD); BENJAMIN MOORE, MONTVALE, N.J. (PAINT); FORMICA, CINCINNATI, N.J., AND WILSONART, TEMPLE, TEXAS (LAMINATES); EAGLE PAINTS, NEW YORK CITY (SPECIAL FINISHES).

32 SAKS FIFTH AVENUE

FIFTH FLOOR MEN'S STORE, UNION SQUARE, SAN FRANCISCO

DESIGN T.S.R. CONSULTANTS, INC., NEW YORK CITY — STEPHEN JOSEPH, VICE PRESIDENT AND PROJECT DIRECTOR/PLANNER; EDWARD CALABRESE, VICE PRESIDENT, AND MATHEW CROWTHER, DESIGN; JOHN HOCH, DIRECTOR CREATIVE RESOURCES, LISA CONTRERAS, CREATIVE RESOURCES, AND MARCYLE WALLMAN, CONSULTANT, ALL FOR COLOR AND MATERIALS; RAJINDER WADHWA, VICE PRESIDENT AND JOB CAPTAIN; DANNY DONG, JOB CAPTAIN; DOMINICK SEGRETE, PRESIDENT AND PARTNER IN CHARGE; SAKS FIFTH AVENUE DESIGN TEAM FRANK KELLAR, VICE PRESIDENT STORE PLANNING AND CONSTRUCTION, HAIG YERANOSSIAN, PLANNER; WALT LICHTENBERG, CONSTRUCTION ADMINISTRATION; ARCHITECT SEGRETE & ROSEN, NEW YORK CITY; CONSULTANTS INTERCITY MECHANICAL, SHERMAN OAKS, CALIF.; MELLEN ELECTRICAL CORP., HEMPSTEAD, N.Y.; WESTCO CONTRACTORS, N. HOLLYWOOD, CALIF.; GENERAL CONTRACTOR HUGHES & COMPANY, DENVER; FIXTURES HUGHES & COMPANY, DENVER (PERIMETER AND LOOSE); M & A WOODWORKING INC., PENSACOLA, FLA. (SHOWCASE AND BACK ISLANDS); FLOORING INNOVATIVE MARBLE & TILE, FARMINGDALE, N.J.; HYDROMENT GROUT, LONG BEACH, CALIF.; PATRICK CARPET MILLS, NEW YORK CITY, AND SUNCRAFT MILLS, NEW YORK CITY (CARPET); MATERIALS VENEER PRODUCTS, LTD., LONG ISLAND CITY, N.Y. (WOOD).

46   SCOTT SHUPTRINE

TROY, MI

DESIGN JON GREENBERG & ASSOCIATES, INC., SOUTHFIELD, MI — ERNIE SZCZERBA, PROJECT SERVICES MANAGER; ELAINE ALBERS, DESIGNER; GREGORY GERALDS, EXECUTIVE DIRECTOR OF PROJECT SERVICES; MIKE O'NEILL, JOB CAPTAIN; GORDON EASON, PROJECT MANAGER; MICHAEL CROSSON, VICE PRESIDENT/PARTNER IN CHARGE; ROBERT BERLIN, SENIOR PROJECT EXECUTIVE; **SCOTT SHUPTRINE DESIGN** MARK MEYER; **CLIENT/OWNER** GARY VAN, TROY, MICH.; **ARCHITECT AND GENERAL CONTRACTOR** JON GREENBERG & ASSOCIATES, INC., SOUTHFIELD, MICH.; **CONSULTANTS** ILLUMINATING CONCEPTS, FARMINGTON HILLS, MICH.; **LIGHTING** CAPRI, LOS ANGELES; REGGIANI, NEW YORK CITY; INFRANOR, WINSTEAD, MINN.; **MILLWORK** MODERN MILLWORK, WIXOM, MICH.; PREMIER CABINETRY, REDFORD TOWNSHIP, MICH.; PATRIE CONSTRUCTION, STERLING HEIGHTS, MICH.; JD&M BUILDING CO., TROY, MICH.; **CEILING** USG INTERIORS INC., CHICAGO; **FIXTURES** MODERN MILLWORK, WIXOM, MICH.; JD&M BUILDING CO., TROY, MICH.; **SIGN** HARMON SIGN CO., TOLEDO, OHIO; **FLOORING** BRUCE HARDWARE FLOORS, WARREN, MICH. (WOOD); VIRGINIA TILE, FARMINGTON HILLS, MICH. (MARBLE); ATLAS CARPET, CITY OF COMMERCE, CALIF. (CARPET); VIRGINIA TILE, FARMINGTON HILLS, MICH., AZROCK, SAN ANTONIO, TEXAS, AND ARMSTRONG, LANCASTER, PA. (TILE); **WALL COVERINGS** SCHUMACHER, NEW YORK CITY; GRAMERCY, NEW YORK CITY; STROHEM & ROMANN, LONG ISLAND CITY, N.Y.; SILK DYNASTY, MOUNTAIN VIEW, CALIF.; THE BLONDER CO., CLEVELAND; KINNEY, CLEVELAND; **MATERIALS** BENJAMIN MOORE, MONTVALE, N.J., AND PITTSBURGH PAINT, PITTSBURGH (PAINT); NEVAMAR, TROY, MICH.; FORMICA, CINCINNATI (LAMINATES); BENZ GLASS CO., DETROIT (GLASS).

144   SIX FLAGS OVER MID-AMERICA

INTERSTATE 44 AND ALLENTON, EUREKA, MO

DESIGN JOHN ROBERTS & ASSOCIATES, SAN FRANCISCO — JAMES C.N. NG, PLANNER, DESIGNER AND PROJECT MANAGER; JIM LOCHE, JOB CAPTAIN; JOHN ROBERTS, PRESIDENT/CEO; **SIX FLAGS OVER MID-AMERICA DESIGN TEAM** LEE GRAHAM, VICE PRESIDENT OF MERCHANDISING; MIKE LEVISON, PARK DESIGN MANAGER; DEBRA ANDERSON AND NICK PITZER, PROJECT TEAM; **CLIENT/OWNER** SIX FLAGS OVER MID-AMERICA (DIVISION OF TIME WARNER); **ARCHITECT** THALDEN CORP., ST. LOUIS; **LIGHTING DESIGNER** JAMES C.N. NG, JOHN ROBERTS & ASSOCIATES; **GENERAL CONTRACTOR** HELMKAMP CONSTRUCTION CO., ST. LOUIS; **LIGHTING** HALO LIGHTING, ELK GROVE VILLAGE, ILL.; **FIXTURING** MIDWEST WOODWORKING & FIXTURE CO., ST. LOUIS; **SPECIAL 3-D FORMS** SPINNAKER DESIGN COLLECTIVE, ST. LOUIS; **FLOORING** DURKAN, DALTON, GA.; **WALL COVERING** ARCHITEX INT'L., CHICAGO; **MATERIALS** FORMICA, CINCINNATI; PIONITE, AUBURN, MAINE (LAMINATES).

98   SPECTRUM MUSIC SUPERSTORE

LYONS CROSSING SHOPPING CENTER, MIAMISBURG, OH

DESIGN THE CHUTE GERDEMAN GROUP, COLUMBUS, OH — BRIAN SHAFLEY, PLANNER, DESIGNER AND VICE PRESIDENT/PARTNER IN CHARGE; BOB WELTY, PLANNER, DESIGNER AND PROJECT MANAGER; MARTA MONSERRATE, DECORATOR; DENNIS C. GERDEMAN, PRESIDENT/CEO; **SPECTRUM MUSIC SUPERSTORE DESIGN TEAM** KENNETH R. CHANCE, DIRECTOR STORE PLANNING; STEVE ROGERS, VISUAL MERCHANDISER; **CLIENT/OWNER** CAMELOT MUSIC, N. CANTON, OHIO; **ARCHITECT** BRUCE PARIS, COLUMBUS, OHIO; **ENGINEERING AND LIGHTING CONSULTANT** GOLIVER AND ASSOC., COLUMBUS, OHIO; **GRAPHIC DESIGNER** LOUIS AND PARTNERS; **GENERAL CONTRACTOR** GAETANO, CANTON, OHIO; **FIXTURES** MARLITE, DOVER, OHIO; TOLEDO STORE FIXTURES, PERRYSBURG, OHIO; BOSTON RETAIL PRODUCTS, BOSTON (MERCHANDISING SYSTEM); **SIGNAGE & GRAPHICS** BLAIR SIGN, ALTOONA, PA.; GRADY MCCAULEY, N. CANTON, OHIO; **A/V EQUIPMENT/LISTENING POSTS** PROGRESSIVE AUDIO, COLUMBUS, OHIO; **FLOORING** TOLI FLOORING, NEW YORK CITY; DURKAN, DALTON, GA. (CARPET).

86   STEUBEN AT THE GREENBRIER

THE GREENBRIER RESORT, WHITE SULPHUR SPRINGS, WV

DESIGN LEE STOUT, INC., NEW YORK CITY — LEE STOUT, CAM LORENDO AND LESLIE STEVEN; **STEUBEN DESIGN TEAM** CHRIS HACKER; STEPHEN BALDWIN AND MATTHEW STEWART (GREENBRIER); **GENERAL CONTRACTOR** THE GREENBRIER, WHITE SULPHUR SPRINGS, W.VA.; **LIGHTING** EDISON PRICE, NEW YORK CITY; HALO, ELK GROVE VILLAGE, ILL.; LIGHTOLIER, SECAUCUS, N.J.; **FURNITURE** ICF, NEW YORK CITY (CHAIRS); **FLOORING** UNITED TILE, NEW YORK CITY (GRANITE); **WALL COVERINGS** MAYA ROMANOFF, CHICAGO; **MATERIALS** DESIGN TEX, NEW YORK CITY, AND ARK BRUMMEL, NEW YORK CITY (FABRIC).

104   TOY WORKS

MALL OF AMERICA, BLOOMINGTON, MN

DESIGN MELVILLE CORP., IN-HOUSE CONSTRUCTION, DESIGN & STORE PLANNING DEPARTMENTS, RYE, N.Y. — ALICE BAYLOG, DIRECTOR OF DESIGN; GARY HUNT, ARCHITECTURAL PROJECT MANAGER; IVANO DIZENZO, EQUIPMENT BUYER; **TOY WORKS' DESIGN TEAM** BRAD ROBINSON, MANAGER OF VISUAL DISPLAY; DONNA CRAWFORD, DIRECTOR OF CONSTRUCTION; **CLIENT/OWNER** KAY BEE TOYS, PITTSFIELD, PA. — TONY PALINO, VICE PRESIDENT/PARTNER IN CHARGE; RON STAFFIERI, PRESIDENT/CEO; **ARCHITECT** MBA ARCHITECT INC., LACROSSE, WIS.; **GRAPHICS CONSULTANT** CRAIG CARL DESIGN, NEW YORK CITY; **LIGHTING CONSULTANT** THOMAS LIGHTING GROUP, TUPELO, MISS.; **GENERAL CONTRACTOR** THE HAHN CO., SAN DIEGO; **LIGHTING** THOMAS INDUSTRIES, TUPELO, MISS.; **FIXTURES** LOZIER FIXTURES, EAST HAMPTON, CONN.; **SIGNAGE** MIDTOWN, NEW YORK CITY; ELECTRA SIGNS, RONKONKOMA, N.Y.

78   WINDSOR FASHIONS

DEL AMO FASHION CENTER, LOS ANGELES

DESIGN CHAIX & JOHNSON, INC., LOS ANGELES — ELIZABETH HOWLEY, PLANNER, DESIGNER, VICE PRESIDENT/PARTNER IN CHARGE AND VICE PRESIDENT/DESIGN; CAROL LEE, DECORATOR; KEITH YAMASAKI, JOB CAPTAIN; SCOTT KOHNO, PRESIDENT/CEO; **DESIGN CONSULTANTS** NICHOLAS ASSOCIATES DESIGN CONSULTANTS, CHICAGO; ; **ARCHITECT** JASON BALINBIN, LOS ANGELES; **STOREFRONT COLUMNS & FRIEZE** ARCHITECTURAL PRODUCTS, N. HOLLYWOOD, CALIF.; **LIGHTING** BOYD LIGHTING, SAN FRANCISCO (WALL SCONCES); **FIXTURES** JEFF TROTT INDUSTRIES, ORANGE, CALIF.; **FURNITURE** NEWMAN FREY, LOS ANGELES (CUSTOM METAL); PIZARRO, MALIBU, CALIF. (FORMAL CHAIRS); **DISPLAY** CALIFORNIA DISPLAY, LOS ANGELES (PLATFORMS/ABSTRACT FORMS); LUNSTEAD METAL, BELLEVUE, WASH. (FORMAL VITRINES); PATINA V, CITY OF INDUSTRY, CALIF. (MANNEQUINS); **SIGNAGE & GRAPHICS** RAZMIK'S DIMENSIONAL GRAPHICS, LOS ANGELES; NICHOLAS ASSOCIATES DESIGN CONSULTANTS, CHICAGO; **FLOORING** GAMMAPAR, LYNCHBURG, VA. (WOOD); WALKER & ZANGER, SUN VALLEY, CALIF. (LIMESTONE FLOOR AND SLATE MOSAIC); TND TILE AND DESIGN, TORRANCE, CALIF. (METALLIC TILE FOR MOSAIC); PACIFIC CREST, IRVINE, CALIF. (FORMAL CARPET); **WALL COVERING** JULIE & JOE STEINBERG, ARTISTS, CHATSWORTH, CALIF. (FAUX PARCHMENT); SARI POLINGER BY INTEX, LOS ANGELES; **MATERIALS** BENJAMIN MOORE, MONTVALE, N.J. (PAINT); ARMSTRONG, LANCASTER, PA. (CEILING TILE).

74   WOLFORD BOUTIQUE

619 MADISON AVENUE, NEW YORK CITY

DESIGN JAMES D'AURIA ASSOCIATES P.C. ARCHITECTS, NEW YORK CITY — JAMES D'AURIA, DESIGNER; JOHN JAMES, SENIOR ASSOCIATE; **CLIENT/OWNER** JAMES CASTY, NEW YORK CITY; **GENERAL CONTRACTOR** HERBERT CONSTRUCTION, NEW YORK CITY; **LIGHTING** LIGHTOLIER, NEW YORK CITY; JAMES D'AURIA ASSOCIATES (CUSTOM WALL SCONCES); **FIXTURES** MEAD AND JOSIPOVICH, NEW YORK CITY; **FLOORING** HOBOKEN WOOD FLOORS, WAYNE, N.J.; DURKAN, NEW YORK CITY (CARPET); **MATERIALS** ROGER ARLINGTON, NEW YORK CITY (DRAPERY FABRIC); **DRAPERY INSTALLATION** REGENCY, NEW YORK CITY.

116   WOOLWORTH'S SOUTH AFRICA

FOURWAYS MALL, JOHANNESBURG, SOUTH AFRICA

DESIGN THE CHUTE GERDEMAN GROUP, COLUMBUS, OH — ELLE CHUTE, PLANNER, DESIGNER, DECORATOR, JOB CAPTAIN, PROJECT MANAGER AND VICE PRESIDENT/PARTNER IN CHARGE; BRIAN SHAFLEY, VICE PRESIDENT DIRECTOR OF DESIGN; DENNIS GERDEMAN, PRESIDENT/CEO; **WOOLWORTH'S DESIGN TEAM** PAUL SIMPSON, COLIN BIRBECK, OHNA DE SWARDT, DEREK PATRICK; **CLIENT/OWNER** WOOLWORTH'S, CAPE TOWN, SOUTH AFRICA; **ARCHITECT** WOOLWORTH'S DESIGN DEPT., CAPE TOWN, SOUTH AFRICA; KAREN SEIDER, JOHANNESBURG, SOUTH AFRICA; **CONSULTANTS** CHORN GOLDMAN WILKINS & ASSOC., JOHANNESBURG, SOUTH AFRICA; **GENERAL CONTRACTOR** AL-CLAD, JOHANNESBURG, SOUTH AFRICA.